Hell: God's Justice, God's Mercy

Challenging the Traditional View of Eternal Torment

Harold R. Eberle

Worldcast Publishing
Yakima, Washington, USA

Hell: God's Justice, God's Mercy
Challenging the Traditional View of Eternal Torment

© 2011 by Harold R. Eberle

Worldcast Publishing
P.O. Box 10653
Yakima, WA 98909-1653
(509) 248-5837
www.worldcastpublishing.com
office@worldcastpublishing.com

ISBN 978-1-882523-29-0
Cover by Lynette Brannan

Table of Contents

Introduction

I believe the Bible is the inspired Word of God and I believe in the existence of hell. However, my study of the Bible leads me to conclude that the wicked people who will be thrown into that terrible place will suffer for the sins they committed and then they will be annihilated—that is, they will burn out of existence.

It takes great care to talk about this subject because some people get defensive when they hear ideas contrary to what they have believed for many years. When people are defensive, they sometimes mishear what is being said. In several meetings I challenged the traditional view of hell, and some people left thinking that I don't believe in hell. That is frustrating because I try to communicate clearly, but the brain is a funny thing. It often inserts words and makes wrong connections when long-held beliefs or issues of the heart are challenged.

For this reason, I want to tell you again that I believe in hell. However, my study of the Bible leads me to embrace the view called annihilationism, which says that the wicked will be annihilated in hell. They will not suffer forever and ever.

There are many Christian leaders who have come to accept this view of hell. For example, in *Universalism and the Doctrine of Hell* (1993), the Anglican leader, John W. Wenham, wrote:

I feel that the time has come when I must declare my mind honestly. I believe that endless torment is a hideous and unscriptural doctrine which has been a terrible burden on the mind of the church and a terrible blot on her presentation of the gospel. I should indeed be happy, if, before I die, I could help in sweeping it away.[1]

In his book *Essentials*, the noted Bible scholar, John Stott wrote that:

the ultimate annihilation of the wicked should at least be accepted as a legitimate, biblically founded alternative to their eternal conscious torment...[2]

The famous hymn writer, Isaac Watts, first believed in the eternal torment of the wicked, but later came to believe that the wicked would be annihilated. The great thinker, Charles Spurgeon, first believed in eternal conscious torment of the wicked, but later came to accept annihilationism as a biblically acceptable view. The American evangelical scholar, Clark Pinnock, stated his belief in annihilationism in a book, entitled *Four Views on Hell*.[3] These and many other Christian leaders have expressed their support of this view.

Before I explain why I embrace this view, let me clearly define what I mean by the word, "hell." Several Bible passages talk about a final judgment day when the wicked will be cast into a place of fire. For example, Jesus explained:

1 John W. Wenham, *Universalism and Doctrine of Hell*, edited by N.M.S. Cameron (Grand Rapids, MI: Baker Book House, 1992), p. xiii.

2 John R. Stott, *Essentials: A Liberal-Evangelical Dialogue* (London: Hodder & Stoughton, 1988), pp. 320-326.

3 3 Clark H. Pinnock, *Four Views of Hell*, edited by William V. Crockett (Grand Rapids, MI: Zondervan Publishing House, 1996), pp.135-174.

"So it will be at the end of the age; the angels will come forth and take out the wicked from among the righteous, and will throw them into the furnace of fire; in that place there will be weeping and gnashing of teeth."

(Matt. 13:49-50)

John refers to this final place of judgment as the "Lake of Fire" (Rev. 20:14-15). It is that Lake of Fire which I will be referring to as hell.

Christians often confuse hades and hell. This confusion is partly because the King James Version of the Bible sometimes translates the Greek word, *hades,* as hell. In reality, hades and hell are two different places. We know this because Revelation 20:11-15 tells us about a future day when hades will be thrown into the Lake of Fire. Most Bible translations (other than the King James Version) recognize this difference between hades and the Lake of Fire. Therefore, they make this distinction obvious by consistently translating the Greek word *hades* with the English word, hades. Hades is the temporary holding place for wicked people until they are cast into hell after the resurrection and the final judgment. I will be using the word hell to refer to that final place of judgment, also called the Lake of Fire.

Let's look into the Bible to learn what will happen to people who are thrown into hell.

Chapter 1

Three Views of Hell

There are three commonly held views of hell: the traditional view, annihilationism, and ultimate reconciliation. Adherents of each view claim that they developed their understanding from the Bible. Yet, their studies resulted in very different understandings.

The *traditional view* is that wicked people will be thrown into hell where they will be tormented, weeping, and gnashing their teeth forever and ever. This suffering is often described as eternal conscious torment.[4]

The second view is called *annihilationism,* which says that people who are thrown into hell will burn out of existence—they will be annihilated.

The third view is called *ultimate reconciliation,*[5] which is the belief that every person who is thrown into hell will eventually repent, be purged of their sins, and then enter into eternal happiness with God and all Christians.

For most of my life I was taught the traditional view and I accepted it without question. After studying this issue for myself, however, I have come to believe that annihilationism is the most biblically accurate position. It will take me several chapters to explain this and to address the pertinent Bible verses, but here I want be sure that I have defined the

---

4 An alternative to this is called the metaphorical view which sees the suffering in hell as spiritual rather than physical.

5 Also referred to as universal reconciliation, universal salvation, or universalism.

three views of hell clearly.

Three Views of Hell

1. *Traditional View:* the wicked will be thrown into hell, where they will weep and gnash their teeth, in pain, forever.

2. *Annihilationism:* the wicked will be thrown into hell and be burned up so that they no longer exist.

3. *Ultimate Reconciliation:* all who are thrown in hell will be purged of evil, until every single person repents and believes in Jesus, to the ultimate end that all will be saved and go to heaven.

Please, allow me to show you why I have come to believe the second view, that God will eventually end the torment of the wicked by putting them out of existence. First, I will contrast annihilationism with the traditional view and then in chapters 10 and 11, I will contrast annihilationism with ultimate reconciliation.

Chapter 2

Will They Burn Forever?

It is Jesus' words which led me to believe that people who are thrown into hell will be annihilated. Our Lord said:

> *"Do not fear those who kill the body but are unable to kill the soul; but rather fear Him who is able to destroy both soul and body in hell."*
>
> (Matt. 10:28)

"To kill" is translated from the Greek word *apokteina*. When applied to the physical body, it means to put to death, slay, or end the life of the body. We have no other interpretation when applied to the soul. To kill the soul means to kill the soul.

In this verse Jesus also warned that God is able *"to destroy both soul and body in hell."* "To destroy" is translated from the Greek word, *apollesai,* and this literally means to completely do away with or to obliterate. So then, if we take this verse literally, we know that God is able to kill and completely destroy the soul and body in hell.

We are also warned that our God is a *Consuming Fire* (Heb. 12:29), and, therefore, it is reasonable to think of His judgment fires as actually consuming rather than tormenting forever.

Clark Pinnock, the prominent evangelical scholar, pointed this out, writing:

The Bible uses the language of *death* and *destruction*, of *ruin* and *perishing*, when it speaks of the fate of the impenitent wicked. It uses the imagery of fire that consumes whatever is thrown into it; linking together images of fire and destruction suggests annihilation.[6]

Supporting this understanding, there are several Bible passages which compare wicked people to chaff that will be burned up on judgment day. For example, Jesus said:

> *"So just as the tares are gathered up and burned with fire, so shall it be at the end of the age. The Son of Man will send forth His angels, and they will gather out of His kingdom all stumbling blocks, and those who commit lawlessness, and will throw them into the furnace of fire..."*
>
> (Matt. 13:40-42)

On judgment day, wicked people will be *"just as the tares"* which are *"burned with fire."*

Similarly, John the Baptist prophesied of the coming judgment saying:

> *"His winnowing fork is in His hand, and He will thoroughly clear His threshing floor; and He will gather His wheat into the barn, but He will burn up the chaff with unquenchable fire."*
>
> (Matt. 3:12)

The wicked are compared with chaff which is consumed when thrown into fire. The implication is that wicked people will be consumed as chaff.

---

6 Clark H. Pinnock, *Four Views of Hell*, edited by William V. Crockett (Grand Rapids, MI: Zondervan Publishing House, 1992), pp.145.

Notice that the fire of hell is called the *"unquenchable fire."* Some readers may take this to mean that people will suffer forever and ever, but that is not implied with this terminology. We can see the fire as unquenchable in the sense that it cannot be put out. This does not mean the fire will burn forever. Even today, firefighters sometimes encounter a building that is burning so ferociously that they cannot quench it. So they simply let the fire burn until it completely burns itself out. This understanding is supported by God's words in Jeremiah 17:27, where He said He would destroy Jerusalem by kindling *"an unquenchable fire."* Indeed, Jerusalem was completely destroyed in 70 AD. No one could quench the fire, but that fire does not burn today. It went out when Jerusalem was utterly destroyed.

Think again of chaff being thrown into fire. In time it is consumed and utterly destroyed. What is the nature of the fire of hell? Does it consume or merely inflict pain without consuming? Our natural experience with fire reveals how it consumes that which is thrown into it. If we see a house on fire, we know that it will be destroyed and only ashes will be left. Even human flesh burns up, rather than remaining alive while burning forever.

Malachi talks about that coming day of judgment, saying:

> *"For behold, the day is coming, burning like a furnace; and all the arrogant and every evildoer will be chaff..."*
>
> (Mal. 4:1)

Peter wrote of the coming judgment day, saying that it will be for the *"destruction of ungodly men"* (II Peter 3:7). The word "destruction" is used rather than "eternal torment." Similarly, Paul wrote that *"their end is destruction"* (Phil. 3:19). Further, he explained that *"...the wages of sin is death...*" (Rom. 6:23). Paul did not say that the wages of sin is eternal torment.

Chapter 3
How Long Will They Burn?

Some Christians who hold the annihilationist view believe that the wicked who will be thrown into hell on judgment day will be burned out of existence instantaneously. Others believe that after the wicked are cast into hell, they will be punished for their sins, and therefore, they will suffer for a period of time before being burned out of existence.

One reason to believe that it will take time for the wicked to burn out of existence is because some Bible verses indicate a coming judgment of varying severity. For example, Jesus told a parable of the future judgment saying:

> *"And that slave who knew his master's will and did not get ready or act in accord with his will, will receive many lashes, but the one who did not know it, and committed deeds worthy of a flogging, will receive but few."*
>
> (Luke 12:47-48)

Such Bible verses reveal that varying punishments await those who live sinful, unrepentant lives. This suggests that the annihilation of the wicked will not be instantaneous. If every wicked person is instantaneously annihilated, then they will all receive the same punishment—then there would be no meaning to the Bible verses which indicate that God will render to every person according to his or her deeds (e.g., Rom.

2:6). So rather than an instantaneous burning out of existence, there may be a period of time during which the wicked will experience true weeping and gnashing of teeth.

Of course, varying punishments may be a result of intensity rather than length of time. If that is true, then all of the sinners may be annihilated rather quickly.

So we do not know *how long* it will take people to burn out of existence. Whether it takes a second or a thousand years for a person to be annihilated, we would be wrong to view hell as an easy way out. God is not mocked. Jesus explained that rather than go to hell, it would be better for a man to pluck out his own eyes or cut off his own hands and feet (Mark 9:43-48). Hell is a terrifying place. Therefore, sinners must not think that judgment will be an easy passage to non-existence. The Bible is very clear that in the flames of fire there will be weeping and gnashing of teeth—real suffering which is to be feared. It will be horrifying.

Chapter 4

The Light Is Judgment

On Judgment Day Jesus will appear in glory and all of humanity—billions of people—will stand before Him. Some Bible passages offer the picture of Jesus separating the righteous from the unrighteous (e.g., Matt. 25:31-32). Other passages seem to indicate that the Light itself will separate the righteous from the unrighteous. For example, our Lord explained:

> *"This is the judgment, that the Light has come into the world, and men loved the darkness rather than the Light, for their deeds were evil. For everyone who does evil hates the Light, and does not come to the Light for fear that his deeds will be exposed. But he who practices the truth comes to the Light, so that his deeds may be manifested as having been wrought in God."*
>
> (John 3:19-21)

This passage can be applied to life everyday because Jesus is the Light right now and at all times. Wicked people who love their sins avoid the revealing of their sins, while the righteous come to the Light of Jesus because they want their sins exposed, forgiven, and cleansed.

Even though the Light of Jesus has already come into the world, Jesus declares that judgment consists of this Light. Therefore, the same Light of Jesus on judgment day will expose all sin. As all of humanity stands before Jesus, He will be revealed in glory and everything will be exposed. Nothing will be hidden in the Light of His glory.

With this understanding, we can see judgment, not as Jesus selecting out individuals and pointing out their sins, but rather as the inevitable outcome of humanity standing in the Light of His glory. In line with this, many leaders in Church history have explained that the Light will be Life to those who long for Him and judgment for those who hate Him.

Supporting this understanding, Jesus said:

> *"He who believes in Him is not judged..."*
>
> (John 3:18)

For those who believe in Jesus, the Light will not be judgment. It will not be a negative experience, but it will be a joyous cleansing. Jesus explained:

> *"But he who practices the truth comes to the Light, so that his deeds may be manifested as having been wrought in God."*
>
> (John 3:21)

The Light of Jesus will actually be attractive and beautiful for all those who believe in Jesus. Therefore, it is a person's response to the Light that will determine their experience of the Light.

Concerning the wicked, Jesus said:

> *"men loved the darkness rather than the Light, for their deeds were evil. For everyone who does evil hates the Light, and does not come to the Light for fear that his deeds will be exposed."*
>
> (John 3:19-20)

Because the wicked hate the Light, they will turn away from the Light. They will cling to their own sins, not wanting to have them revealed, forgiven, and cleansed. They love their own sins and darkness. As a consequence, wicked people will actually choose darkness over the Light. They will choose to go to hell rather than be with Jesus.

Yet, the Light of Jesus will continue to be revealed and it will fill all and be in all. Therefore, even that which was dark will be filled with the Light of His Glory. As the wicked cling to their own sins, they will be consumed in the Glory of God. Hence, they will be annihilated like chaff that is burned in fire.

Chapter 5

Conditional Immortality

The question of whether or not wicked people will suffer in hell forever hinges on the basic nature of humanity. Only if people are immortal beings can they—and will they—remain alive forever while suffering in hell.[7] If people are mortal, then we may expect the fire of judgment to end their existence. So, then, are people mortal or immortal?

Most modern-day Christians were taught that the souls of all people—the righteous and the unrighteous—will exist forever. This is the traditional view of humanity's existence. Let's challenge this traditional view.

After Adam sinned, God told him:

> *"For you are dust,*
> *And to dust you shall return."*
>
> (Gen. 3:19)

Some teachers try to explain this as only referring to Adam's physical body, but God directed this toward Adam. He said "you" shall return to dust. Furthermore, God closed off the tree of life, so that Adam would not eat from it and then live forever:

> *"and now, he might stretch out his hand, and take*

---

7 An alternative view which some traditionalists hold is that the wicked are mortal, but God will supernaturally sustain them forever while they suffer in hell.

also from the tree of life, and eat, and live forever."

(Gen. 3:22)

Notice here the possibility for Adam to live forever. This means he was not already in a condition to live forever. This refers to his entire being.

If Adam ate from the tree of life, he would be immortal. We can partake of Jesus, and hence, become immortal. It is the life of God that makes us immortal. The Bible clearly declares that God alone is immortal. Paul writes in I Timothy about God *"who alone possesses immortality"* (I Tim. 6:16). Humans only become immortal when they access the divine nature of God, through Jesus Christ.

This is a central feature of the Gospel.

> *And the testimony is this, that God has given us eternal life, and this life is in His Son. He who has the Son has the life; he who does not have the Son of God does not have the life.*

(I John 5:11-12)

A person who does not have Jesus does not possess within them eternal life.

This understanding, that only believers in Jesus are immortal, is called *conditional immortality*. Theologians refer to it by this name because there is a condition on being immortal. That condition is receiving the eternal life of God through Jesus Christ.

Some teachers use the terms "conditional immortality" and "annihilationism" interchangeably, but the focus is slightly different. Conditional immortality refers to the nature of humanity, conditional upon one's acceptance or rejection of Jesus Christ. Annihilationism refers to the nature of hell and the fires of hell having the ability to consume that which is thrown in there. These two doctrines are compatible with one another because non-Christians do not have eternal life, and therefore, they will be burned out of existence in hell.

E.G. Selwyn, the Dean of Winchester, wrote:

> There is little in the NT to suggest a state of everlasting punishment, but much to indicate an ultimate destruction or dissolution of those who cannot enter into life: conditional immortality seems to be the doctrine most consonant with the teaching of Scripture.[8]

Because conditional immortality is compatible with annihilationism, it is worth confirming with more Bible passages that eternal life is conditioned upon receiving Jesus Christ. Consider our Lord's words:

> *"Truly, truly, I say to you, he who hears My word, and believes Him who sent Me, has eternal life, and does not come into judgment, but has passed out of death into life."*
>
> (John 5:24)

Then again:

> *"He who believes in the Son has eternal life; but he who does not obey the Son will not see life, but the wrath of God abides on him."*
>
> (John 3:36)

What I hope you can accept is that the definition of "eternal life" is "eternal life." This may seem simplistic, but many

---

8 Edward G. Selwyn, *The First Epistle of St. Peter* (London: Macmillian, 1961), p. 358.

Christians were taught that eternal life is a certain God-like quality of life. Of course, we become partakers of divine life when we receive Jesus Christ; however, that life also provides eternal existence.

Finally, consider the most known verse in the Bible, John 3:16:

> *"For God so loved the world, that He gave His only begotten Son, that whoever believes in Him shall not perish, but have eternal life."*

Those who are not saved will *"perish."* This means they will "cease to exist." Those who do believe in Jesus have eternal life.

Chapter 6

Doctrine of Immortality

Traditional Christianity teaches that all people—the righteous and the unrighteous—will live forever, either in heaven or hell. Now that I challenge this doctrine, it is worth considering why so many Christians today think that all people are immortal beings.

The Bible never says that the souls of people are immortal (apart from the life of Jesus Christ). It tells us the opposite:

> *For the fate of the sons of men and the fate of beasts is the same. As one dies so dies the other; indeed, they all have the same breath...All go to the same place. All came from the dust and all return to the dust.*
>
> (Eccl. 3:19-20)

Some Christians may try to explain away such Bible passages claiming that they are only referring to the physical body, but they would not come to that conclusion if they did not already hold to the doctrine of the immortality of the human soul. A reading of these Scriptures without any preconceived ideas leads the reader to understand that people in their natural state are mortal.

The Psalmist tells us the same truth:

> *Do not trust in princes,*

In mortal man, in whom there is no salvation.
His spirit departs, he returns to the earth;
In that very day his thoughts perish.

(Ps. 146:3-4)

People's *"thoughts perish,"* meaning more than physical death is involved.

The apostle Paul writes about the rewards awaiting those who *"by perseverance in doing good seek for glory and honor and immortality..."* (Rom. 2:7). It would make no sense for Paul to encourage us to seek for immortality, if we already possessed it. The obvious point is that people (without the life of Jesus) are mortal.

Since the Bible tells us this, why do so many Christians today believe that all people—the righteous and the unrighteous—will live forever?

When we study Church history we learn that ancient Greek philosophy had a profound influence upon early Christianity. The ancient Greek philosophers (e.g., Plato and Aristotle) believed that people always existed and always will exist. Their concept of humanity was that each person exists as a spirit being in eternity, but each person descends into a physical body to inhabit and dwell on earth for a time. At physical death, they leave their bodies and go on living in a spiritual state eternally.

Some of the early Church leaders were influenced greatly by this Greek way of thinking. Although the concept of people pre-existing (existing in eternity past) was rejected by most of the early Church, many embraced the idea that all people go on living forever. By the fourth century most of the Church was teaching the immortality of all people.

Dr. William Temple, the late Archbishop of Canterbury, Primate of Great Britain, wrote:

If men had not imported the Greek and unbiblical notion [from Plato], of the natural indestruction of the individual soul, and then read the New Testament with that already in their minds, they would have drawn from it a belief, not in everlasting torment, but in annihilation.[9]

Before the influence of Greek philosophy, the early Church did not commonly believe that people are eternal beings. Some scholars who study the writings of the early Church fathers concluded that Clement of Rome, Ignatius, Polycarp, and Irenaeus each believed that wicked people will go out of existence. Others scholars who study these writings will debate some of these findings; however, there is no doubt that at least Irenaeus was firm on the mortality of humanity— soul and body.[10]

Consider the Jewish religious leaders in Jesus' day. The Sadducees concluded from their study of the Old Testament that people's existence ended when they died physically (Luke 20:27). Most of the Pharisees, on the other hand, believed that the dead would be resurrected from the grave by the power of God. When Jesus talked with the Jewish religious leaders on this subject, He explained:

"The sons of this age marry and are given in marriage, but those who are considered worthy to attain to that age and the resurrection from the dead, neither marry, nor are given in marriage; for they cannot even die anymore, because they are like angels, and are sons of God, being sons of the

9 William Temple, *Christian Faith and Life* (London: SCM Press Ltd., 1954), p. 81.

10 For a list of dozens of Church leaders who believe in conditional immortality, see: http://www.specialtyinterests.net/champions_of_conditional_immortality.html

resurrection."

(Luke 20:34b-36)

Notice Jesus did not say everyone is immortal. On the contrary, He taught that only those worthy of the resurrection would be as the angels. Only those who are sons of God cannot *"die anymore."*

In another passage Jesus said:

> *"an hour is coming, in which all who are in the tombs will hear His voice, and will come forth; those who did the good deeds to a resurrection of life, those who committed the evil deeds to a resurrection of judgment."*

(John 5:28-29)

From this we know that there will be a future resurrection of the righteous and the unrighteous. We are told that only the righteous will experience life. The wicked will experience judgment.

What is that judgment? They will be thrown into the Lake of Fire where they will be punished for their sins and then burn out of existence. The wicked will be burned out of existence because they are not immortal beings.

Chapter 7

The Traditionalist's Verses

If I hold to the doctrine of annihilationism with integrity then I must deal with the specific Bible passages which are used by others to teach the traditional view of hell that wicked people will be in eternal conscious torment. Let's look at those passages in this chapter and the one to follow.

There are two passages from the book of Revelation that traditionalists like to use to support their doctrine. The apostle John wrote:

> *And the devil who deceived them was thrown into the lake of fire and brimstone, where the beast and the false prophet are also; and they will be tormented day and night forever and ever.*
>
> (Rev. 20:10)

The reason this verse does not support the doctrine of everlasting torment is because the phrase *"forever and ever"* was translated from the Greek words, *aionios aionon*. Let's look carefully at these Greek words.

The Greek root word, *aion*, is literally translated as "age" or "dispensation of time." The Greek words, *aion* and *aionios*, can be difficult to translate because an age or dispensation of time can vary in length. The age in which God dwells is eternal, but there are other ages which are limited in time. There are ages of the Gentiles, ages when the Jews lived in God's favor and ages when the Jews were out of God's favor. There are ages long past and ages pertaining to the future.

Therefore, *aion* can refer to forever or it may be any long, indefinite length of time. For this reason, *aion* (along with the various endings which indicate a specific part of speech in the Greek language) is sometimes translated with words indicating unending time, such as "forever," "everlasting" or "eternal." In other contexts, *aion* is translated with words which are more vague, but implying a period of time having an end and/or a beginning.

A good example is seen in Titus 1:2, where the Greek word, *aionion,* is used twice:

> *in the hope of* [aionion] *eternal life, which God, who cannot lie, promised long* [aionion] *ages ago.*

Both times, *aionion* pertains to a dispensation of time, but two different dispensations are being referred to. The dispensation during which Christians will live with God will be everlasting, therefore, *aionion* has been translated as "eternal." But the other dispensation referred to in this verse ended in the distant past. Therefore, *aionion* has been translated as "ages ago."

The apostle Paul also talks about a dispensation with an ending:

> *Now these things happened to them as an example, and they were written for our instruction upon whom the end of the* [aionon] *ages have come.*
>
> (1 Cor. 10:11)

Again, we seen how *aion* refers to an age or a dispensation, but the context tells us how long that dispensation lasts.

Another place where *aion* refers to a limited dispensation of time is in Matthew 24:3, where the disciples asked Jesus about the end of the age:

> *"Tell us, when will these things happen, and what will be the sign of Your coming, and of the end of the* [aionos] *age?"*

There cannot be an *"end of the age"* if *aionos* means forever. The King James Version translates this phrase as *"end of the world,"* which again reveals a period of time that has an ending to it.

Now let's consider the Bible passages in which the two Greek words, *aionios aionon,* are put together. They are often translated as "ages of ages." They can also be translated literally as "dispensations of dispensations."

How long is ages of ages? It depends upon which ages of ages a person is talking about. The ages of ages in which God dwells are eternal. Where ages of ages are spoken of in other contexts, they may refer to any long, indefinite period of time.

With this understanding we can see that the Bible translators had to make a judgment call each time they came across the Greek words *aionios aionon.* If they translated these words as "ages of ages," then they left the reader to decide, but when they assigned a specific period of time, then they decided what they thought best fit the context.

Look again at Revelation 20:10:

> *And the devil who deceived them was thrown into the lake of fire and brimstone, where the beast and the false prophet are also; and they will be tormented day and night* [aionios aionon] *forever and ever.*

This translation tells us more about the translators than it does about the meaning intended by the original writer. If the translators had no preconceived ideas about how long torment will be in hell, then they would have said the devil, the beast, and false prophet will be tormented day and night, for ages of ages. But since they translated *aionios aionon* as "forever and ever" we know that the translators already held to the traditional doctrine of hell.

Because *aionios aionon* does not specifically tell us how long the ages are, Revelation 20:10 does not actually tell us how long people will suffer in hell.

Furthermore, Revelation 20:10 only talks about the devil, the beast, and the false prophet; we know that the devil is a spiritual being, and we are not sure if the beast and the false prophet are human beings. Many scholars believe that the beast is the personification of a totalitarian political system. The false prophet of Revelation may represent the voice of a false religious system rather than an individual. Acknowledging this, we realize that Revelation 20:10 does not tell us anything about how long *people* will suffer in hell.

Now consider the other passage in the book of Revelation that traditionalists like to use to support their doctrine:

> *"If anyone worships the beast and his image, and receives a mark on his forehead or on his hand... he will be tormented with fire and brimstone in the presence of the holy angels and in the presence of the Lamb. And the smoke of their torment goes up forever and ever; they have no rest day and night, those who worship the beast and his image, and whoever receives the mark of his name."*
>
> (Rev. 14:9-11)

We already explained how *"forever and ever,"* was translated from *aionios aionon,* which does not necessarily mean forever and it is literally translated as, "ages of ages."

It is also worth noting how Christians who use this passage to argue for the doctrine of eternal torment focus on the phrase: *"their torment goes up forever and ever."* But actually it does not say their torment will last forever and ever, but rather, it says the *"smoke"* of their torment goes up forever and ever. What is meant by this smoke?

The book of Revelation is a very symbolic book, using apocalyptic language. "Smoke" sometimes refers to how things would vanish and *only the memory of those things would remain.* Such apocalyptic language was commonly used in declarations of judgment and end times.

To confirm this, we can see how the same terminology is used elsewhere in the Bible. In fact, the writer of Revelation may have borrowed the words of Isaiah as recorded in Isaiah 34:8-10:

> *For the Lord has a day of vengeance,*
> *A year of recompense for the cause of Zion.*
> *Its streams will be turned into pitch,*
> *And its loose earth into brimstone,*
> *And its land will become burning pitch.*
> *It will not be quenched night or day;*
> *Its smoke will go up forever.*
> *From generation to generation it will be desolate;*

In this passage, Isaiah was declaring the coming destruction of the city of Bozrah and the land of Edom. Isaiah said that the *"smoke will go up forever,"* but this did not mean that fire would continue destroying the region forever. We know this because Isaiah went on to say:

> *But pelican and hedgehog will possess it,*
> *And owl and raven will dwell in it...*

> *Thorns will come up in its fortified towers,*
> *Nettles and thistles in its fortified cities;*
> *It will be a haunt of jackals...*
>
> (Is. 34:11-13)

Since wild animals and plants were to take over the land, we must conclude that the phrase, *"smoke going up forever,"* did not mean that fire would continue burning forever. Rather, it meant that what existed in the land would only be a memory. The land itself would be left desolate.

For further evidence of this we can read Revelation 19 which tells us about the judgment of Babylon:

> *Her smoke rises up forever and ever.*
>
> (Rev. 19:3)

In the same context, we are told that Babylon will *"be burned up with fire,"* (Rev. 18:8) *"and will not be found any more"* (Rev. 18:21). Hence, we see "smoke," not as a sign of ongoing pain, but rather as the only thing left after judgment is complete. Babylon, we are told will vanish and only the memory will remain.

Therefore, when we read Revelation 14:9-11, we should understand that people who received the mark of the beast will be annihilated and only a memory or a scent of them will remain. So then, rather than support the traditionalist's view, this passage actually supports annihilationism.

Chapter 8

What Is Eternal Judgment?

There are three more Bible passages which traditionalists like to use to support their doctrine of everlasting torment in hell. Let's examine those passages now.

The King James Version of Matthew 25:46, says:

> *"And these shall go away into* [aionion] *everlasting punishment: but the righteous into life* [aionion] *eternal."*

If, indeed, the wicked will go away into everlasting punishment, then the traditionalists are correct—hell will entail forever torment. But the word "everlasting" is translated from the Greek word, *aionion*. Rather than tell us that hell is forever, this tells us that the translators who developed the King James Version already held to the traditional view of hell.

This doctrinal bias is confirmed when we see that *aionion* is translated in two different ways within this one verse, first as everlasting and second as eternal. By saying that the wicked go away into [*aionion*] everlasting punishment, the translators were leading the reader to only one conclusion— that hell will entail forever torment. But, as explained in the preceding chapter, *aionion* literally refers to a dispensation of time. It can mean everlasting, but it can also mean a dispensation of time which will have an end.

We know that the King James translators understood this because they translated *aionion* in other ways in other passages. For example, the King James Version of Romans 16:25, says:

> the preaching of Jesus Christ, according to the revelation of the mystery, which was kept secret [aionios] *since the world began.*

"Since the world began" is not forever and ever. Similarly, in II Tim. 1:9, the KJV translators translated *aionion* as *"before the world began."* And in Titus 1:2, as *"before the beginning of time."*

The translators of the New American Standard Version were consistent in translating the Greek word *aionion* both times it is used in Matthew 25:46:

> *"These will go away into* [aionion] *eternal punishment, but the righteous into* [aionion] *eternal life."*
>
> (Matt. 25:46)

We can commend the translators of the New American Standard Version for being consistent. However, we still must keep in mind that the word *aionion* does not necessarily mean "eternal."

Even if we accept this word "eternal" as the best translation, we must also consider how the words "eternal punishment," do not necessarily mean "eternal punishing." The second implies ongoing torment forever and ever. But the first, "eternal punishment," may indicate an event with eternal consequences.

Please consider this seriously. "Eternal punishment" may indicate the eternal judgment, in the sense of being the final judgment. It will be a judgment from which no one can appeal. It will be a judgment which shall never be reversed. Eternal judgment will be ultimate destruction. This understanding sees that people will be judged and God's sentencing will be final—never to change. Christians who believe in annihilationism understand this to be the actual meaning of "eternal judgment" or "eternal punishment."

Now look at another verse which traditionalists like to use to support their doctrine of everlasting torment. In 2 Thessalonians 1:9, we are told about the destiny of those who are disobedient to the gospel:

> *These will pay the penalty of eternal destruction, away from the presence of the Lord and from the glory of His power.*

Annihilationists, such as myself, like to point out that *"eternal destruction"* does not necessarily entail torment which goes on forever.

For further clarification, we can note that "eternal" in this verse is translated from the Greek word, *aionion*. In this and other passages *aionion* is used to modify words such as, "destruction," "fire," "punishment" or "judgment." In the verse we just quoted, *aionion* modifies "destruction." This does not necessarily indicate a destruction that goes on forever, but it can refer to an event with eternal consequences. It is an eternal destruction in the sense that it is the final destruction.

This view is supported by other Bible verses. For example, Jude verse 7, tells us that Sodom and Gomorrah were destroyed by *"eternal fire."* Even though the fire is called "eternal," the fire which destroyed Sodom and Gomorrah is not burning today. That fire went out many years ago. It was eternal in the sense that it brought ultimate and final destruction upon Sodom and Gomorrah.

There is one more passage that traditionalists common-ly use to support their doctrine of everlasting torment. It is Mark 9:47-48, where our Lord warned:

"If your eye causes you to stumble, throw it out; it is better for you to enter the kingdom of God with one eye, than having two eyes, to be cast into hell, where their worm does not die, and the fire is not quenched."

Traditionalists read this Scripture (or Mark 9:44-46, which is similar) and conclude that wicked people will never die.

In chapter 2, we talked about the unquenchable fire, and we saw how this means that the fire cannot be quenched. But just because the fire cannot be extinguished does not mean that people who are thrown into that fire will burn forever.

Now consider how Jesus referred to the worm which *"does not die."* Traditionalists often think of this worm as the soul of a person which will wiggle in pain forever and ever in hell. In reality, the worm in this passage is *not* correlated with a person's soul. The worm is correlated with a worm that at-tacks a dead body and eats it. The worm is properly under-stood as a maggot that eats a corpse.

We know this because our Lord was quoting this phrase from Isaiah 66:23b-24, where God's judgment is described:

"All mankind will come to bow down before Me,"
    says the Lord.
"Then they shall go forth and look
On the corpses of the men
Who have transgressed against Me.
For their worm will not die
And their fire shall not be quenched..."

The "worm" works in unison with the "fire." Both will consume.

The worm (maggot) is not likened to the person, but the maggot comes from outside and eats the person. By saying the maggot will not die, Jesus was declaring that wicked people will not be able to outlive their devourers. With this understanding, we can see how the wicked people eventually will be burned, eaten, or consumed, even though the maggot may go on living just as the fire of hell goes on burning.[11]

There! We have just explained the passages which traditionalists like to use to "prove" their doctrine of eternal torment. None of the passages actually say what the traditionalists claim. In fact, annihilationists like to point out that the traditionalists have no verse which clearly states that hell entails everlasting torment, but there are several verses which do clearly state that people will be killed, destroyed, and burned like chaff.

---

11 An alternative understanding of this passage held by many Bible teachers is that the destruction being referred to here is the destruction which occurred when Jerusalem was destroyed in 70 A.D. At that time, thousands of people were thrown beyond the walls of Jerusalem into the burning, maggot-ridden rubbish heap called *gehenna*.

Chapter 9

Do Christians Really Believe?

The traditionalist's doctrine of hell is used by atheists more than any other doctrine to ridicule Christianity. This is no reason for us to reject the doctrine, but it should give us reason to reconsider if the doctrine is logical. Is it scriptural? We should also ask ourselves if we really believe it.

Christians who say they believe the doctrine of eternal torment do not live as if it is true. Please let me explain.

What would you do if some unsaved person whom you love was in the hospital about to die? If you truly believed the eternal torment doctrine, then you would hurry to warn them about the coming judgment. But your loved-one is not the only person about to die. The hospitals are filled with unsaved people soon to take their last breath.

Compare this reality to watching your neighborhood burn to the ground. If you honestly believed that a huge fire was about to consume your neighborhood, you would get up from your chair right now and run to help. You would call the fire department; you would yell out to warn your neighbors or actually do something heroic to try to save them. Yet, a fire in the neighborhood pales into insignificant when compared with what traditional Christians say they believe about hell—billions and billions of people forever weeping and gnashing their teeth.

If you truly believe that after ten trillion years of agony people in hell will only have begun their suffering, then you better get busy. In fact, you should not be wasting time relaxing, eating, sleeping, or reading this book. If hell is forever pain and you have the answers for people, then you better spend every waking moment of the rest of your life warning others. To do otherwise would not only be unloving; it would be cruel and evil.

Of course, there are some evangelists who frequently remind themselves of hell's future torment. Indeed, this vision helps motivate them to carry on with their work. I am grateful for what they do. I, too, spend much time in evangelistic work. But even the most aggressive evangelists do not give every waking moment to warning people. Even they do not live consistently with the traditional view of hell.

I can't live my life with such inconsistency. It is too hard to embrace the Church's traditional teaching about hell and still live a normal life. How can I work, mow my lawn, or raise my children if most of the world is headed toward such an eternity? I can't do it and I don't see any other Christians capable of living with that awareness either. They go on vacations. They relax in front of the television. They laugh and have good times. They may say that they believe in a future judgment bringing the eternal torment of all non-Christians, but none of them seems to *really* believe it.

The eternal torment doctrine seems to me to be just a "pretend doctrine." I do not want to offend traditionalists, but I don't think I have ever met a Christian who actually lives as if this doctrine is true. If someone truly believed the eternal torment doctrine they would have to be a neurotic evangelist or they would have to be extremely cold-hearted. John Stott said it well:

> I find the concept intolerable and do not understand how people can live with it without either cauterizing their feelings or cracking under the strain.[12]

---

12 Stott, *Essentials*, p. 314.

Think seriously about the position of a Christian who believes the eternal torment doctrine. Compare that position to the wealthy individual in India who walks the streets everyday past the crippled, blind, and hungry. To the on-looker it is difficult to understand how someone can be so cold-hearted as to walk by without extending a helping hand. Yet, that cold-heartedness is trivial compared with what is being done everyday by the Christian who believes the eternal torment doctrine.

I am not someone who can pretend believing in one doctrine while living my daily life inconsistent with that doctrine. I can't sit still or sleep at night until I have resolved such conflicts. So I studied the Bible carefully and I have come to believe that the wicked people who will be thrown into hell will be punished for their sins, but they will eventually burn out of existence. I also believe in a God who is merciful. I cannot believe that God who loved humanity so much that He sent His Son to die for us, is the same god who would torture people forever. That is not who God is.

Chapter 10

Ultimate Reconciliation

It is time to turn our attention to the third view of hell, called ultimate reconciliation.[13] This is the belief that all human beings will be reconciled to God; that is, all people ultimately will go to heaven. Hell is not seen as a place of punishment, but rather purification. Some advocates go so far as to say that Satan and all the demons will some day see the light, repent, and be saved.

In order to embrace the view of ultimate reconciliation one must accept the idea that people can be saved after they die (post mortem). God is not limiting the opportunities for salvation for this lifetime. According to ultimate reconciliationists many post-mortem conversions will take place the instant people see Jesus after they die. However, some ultimate reconciliationists propose that the vast majority of sinners will repent during the period of the new heavens and the new earth described in Revelation 21 and 22.

Revelation 21 describes New Jerusalem coming down out of heaven from God. Jesus dwells in Jerusalem and from there the light of His glory radiates outward. Those who live within Jerusalem will constantly bathe in the eternal presence of God. They are the ones whose names are written in the book of Life. But outside of New Jerusalem there are multitudes of people; the farther they get from New Jerusalem the darker

---

13 Also referred to as universal reconciliation, universal salvation, or universalism.

it becomes. Some even live in the outer darkness, completely away from the presence of the Lord. They will suffer for their sins, but God will continue revealing His love and drawing them to Himself.

According to Revelation 21:25, the gates of the city are never closed. Ultimate reconciliationists take this to mean that people can repent at any time. No one unclean will enter the city, but once they do repent they are welcome into the presence of Jesus. Revelation 21:26 shows us a constant stream of people bringing the glory of the nations into the city, meaning that people are constantly turning to Jesus and drawing near to Him. According to the ultimate reconciliationist, each and every person will eventually repent, be purged of their sins, and enter into eternal happiness with Jesus.

I have several friends who hold to this view of ultimate reconciliation or some variation of this view. Although I disagree with them, I recognize that they are Christians who believe in Jesus as their Lord and Savior. Ultimate reconciliation was held by several of the early Church fathers including Clement of Alexandria, Origen, and St. Gregory of Nyssa. Some popular modern teachers of ultimate reconciliation include Carlton Pearson, Thomas Talbott, Stephen Jones, J. Preston Eby, and Gregory MacDonald.

Ultimate reconcilationists use certain Bible passages to support their position. One of their favorite verses is I John 2:2:

> and He Himself is the propitiation for our sins; and not for ours only, but also for those of the whole world.

Through the reconcilationist's eyes, this verse declares that Jesus paid for all people's sins, and therefore, all people will be saved.

Another favorite verse of ultimate reconciliationists is Colossians 1:20:

> *and through Him to reconcile all things to Him-*
> *self, having made peace through the blood of His*
> *cross; through Him, I say, whether things on earth*
> *or things in heaven.*

Reconciliationists like to point out how this verse says *"all things"* will be reconciled.

Being someone who does not believe in ultimate reconciliation, I can point out some of the errors of their thinking. For example, Colossians 1:20, which I just quoted, says *"things on earth and things in heaven"* will be reconciled to God; it does not say things in hell will be reconciled.

I also quoted I John 2:2, where John tells us that Jesus is the propitiation for the sins of the whole world, but three verses earlier we are told that sins must be confessed and forgiveness received (I John 1:9). So even if Jesus made provision for the forgiveness of all people's sins, this is no guarantee that His forgiveness will be appropriated. One does not necessarily follow the other.

We must also look carefully at the ultimate reconciliationist's understanding of what will happen on the new earth. They envision that Lake of Fire as somewhere outside the city Jerusalem, yet still on Earth. Hence, they see that people will be able to move from the Lake of Fire into Jerusalem and into the presence of Jesus.

That explanation does not match what is actually described in Revelation 20-23. In chapter 20, the great judgment takes place and all whose names are not written in the book of Life are cast into the Lake of Fire. Then after that great judgment, Revelation 21 tells us about a new heaven and new earth. Note the sequence of events. First, the wicked are cast away into the Lake of Fire (hell) and then the new heaven and earth come. This implies that the Lake of Fire is not on the new earth. It is somewhere else. The Lake of Fire seems to be a completely different location separate from the new earth and even existing before the new earth.

There is no evidence that those who are in the Lake of Fire will be able to move from that location to New Jerusalem. We do have biblical evidence that those on the new earth may move into New Jerusalem, but they are already on the new earth, not in the Lake of Fire.

There are other verses which reconciliationists like to use to support their doctrine and many books have been written to discuss the counter arguments. Here I will simply point out three Scriptures that to me cannot be reconciled with the view of ultimate reconciliation.

First, Paul writes of the coming judgment:

> *when the Lord Jesus will be revealed from heaven with His mighty angels in flaming fire, dealing out retribution to those who do not know God and to those who do not obey the gospel of our Lord Jesus. These will pay the penalty of eternal destruction....*
> (II Thes. 1:6-9)

This verse clearly tells of eternal destruction, not ultimate reconciliation.

A second passage which cannot be reconciled with ultimate reconciliation is Hebrews 11:26-27:

> *For if we go on sinning willfully after receiving the knowledge of the truth, there no longer remains a sacrifice for sins, but a terrifying expectation of judgment and the fury of a fire which will consume the adversaries.*

This idea that there *"no longer remains a sacrifice for sins"* contradicts that idea of ultimate reconciliationists that Jesus' death will take care of all people's sins.

Finally, Matthew 12:32 says:

> *Whoever speaks a word against the Son of Man, it*
> *shall be forgiven him; but whoever speaks against*
> *the Holy Spirit, it shall not be forgiven him, either*
> *in this age or in the age to come.*

Mark 3:28-29 also talks about this sin against the Holy Spirit and says that it will *never* been forgiven. This warning about the unforgiveable sin does not fit well with the ultimate reconciliationist's view. Of course, ultimate reconciliationists have an answer for this and they will usually say that those who commit the unforgiveable sin will still make it to heaven, yet with a stain of sin always remaining on their soul.

To me this explanation is unacceptable, because I cannot conceive of a person living in the fullness of God's presence eternally while still having the stain and guilt of sin. This being true, I cannot accept the idea that all of humanity will ultimately be reconciled to God.

Chapter 11
Nature of God and Humanity

We have noted some of the errors of ultimate reconciliation. It is just as important that we recognize how that view is also in conflict with the nature of God and the nature of humanity as revealed in Scripture. Please let me explain.

Christians who hold to ultimate reconciliation understand that God's judgment is not "punitive," meaning it is not for the purpose of punishing sin. Rather, reconcilationists see judgment as "remedial," referring to how God's judgment is only to remedy the problem of sin. In order to support their view of judgment, they like to point out the laws in the Old Testament that were for the purpose of remedying rather than punishing. For example, when a man killed a neighbor's ox, he was expected to replace the ox. In such a situation the man was not punished, but rather expected to right the wrong. Ultimate reconciliationists see the judgment of God in similar fashion. Judgment, then, is for the purpose of fixing a person, cleansing him, and reconciling him to God. It is thought that in the Light of Jesus everyone will want to repent and believe.

This may sound wonderful at first and, indeed, it is comforting to think that all of humanity will eventually come to God. However, we need to seriously consider God's role in judgment. Do the Scriptures reveal that judgment will be punitive or remedial? Will God actually punish evil or will He simply right the wrongs?

In reality, God's judgment is a pervasive theme throughout Scripture. Two glaring examples stand out: Noah's flood and the destruction of Sodom and Gomorrah. These judgments were not to remedy the circumstances but they had terminal consequences.

Another revealing example of God's judgment is seen when the Hebrew people rebelled against God and made a molten calf to worship. God said, *"Whoever has sinned against Me, I will blot him out of My book"* (Ex. 32:33). In this case, God did not reveal Himself just so people would repent. He inflicted a punishment which had eternal consequences.

The New Testament warns us that past judgments reveal how God will deal with wicked people in the future (Jude vs. 5-7). The wrath of God is a real aspect of His nature to be feared. To many He will say, *"I never knew you; depart from Me, you who practice lawlessness"* (Matt. 7:23). God is referred to as a Consuming Fire, implying that He will indeed consume in the sense of destroying all that is evil. Peter wrote of the coming judgment day, saying that it will be for the *"destruction of ungodly men"* (II Peter 3:7). Note that the judgment day is not for the reconciliation of ungodly men, but for their destruction.

Another reason we must reject the view of ultimate reconciliation is that it changes one's concept of humanity. Just as the traditionalists, they take from Greek philosophy the idea that all people are immortal beings. This negates the Scriptures which tell us that people receive eternal life only if and when they receive Jesus Christ.

In addition, the reconciliationist sees people as simply beings in different stages of development; some will be saved now and others will be saved later. This viewpoint denies the fundamental differences within people. Jesus explained that evil people *hate* the light, while believers come to the light (John 3:20-21). Ultimate reconciliationists lose this truth.

They cannot see the clear difference between Christians and non-Christians. Some people have been born again into the family of God and some have not. There is a distinction. The coming judgment is based on this distinction. Our Lord made it very clear what awaits the sinner and what awaits the righteous (i.e., Matt. 13:37-43; Matt. 25:31-46; John 5:28-29). There is coming a separation between the wicked and the righteous.

Furthermore, people have a free will. Ultimate reconciliationists make no room for the possibility that people can choose to not repent.

So, then, we can see that adopting the view of ultimate reconciliation entails more than accepting a certain view of hell. It requires the acceptance of a view of God which minimizes His role as a Judge and Consuming Fire. It also changes one's concept of humanity, seeing all people as individuals at different stages of becoming good, rather than recognizing that some people are actually evil and they choose evil.

Of course, God wants all people to come to Him. However, He will not force people to receive His love. A day will come when He separates the sheep from the goats. There will be a final judgment.

Chapter 12

Our Concept of God

The most important reason that we should resolve this question about the nature of hell is because of the implications it has upon our concept of God.

Today we have preachers at opposite ends of a spectrum. Some preachers want to talk about the love of God and they see God's judgments as an embarrassment. Others think they are speaking on behalf of God only when they are breathing fire and brimstone. I find ultimate reconciliation and the traditional view of hell at these two extremes and neither extreme offers an accurate view of God.

An accurate view is offered by God as He revealed Himself on Mount Sinai saying:

> *"The LORD, the LORD God, compassionate and gracious, slow to anger, and abounding in loving-kindness...yet He will by no means leave the guilty unpunished..."*
>
> (Ex. 34:6-7)

God is full of goodness. He is love. Yet, there is also an aspect of His nature to be feared by those who live in disobedience to Him.

So then, what view of hell corresponds to this biblical revelation of God?

From my study, I conclude that ultimate reconciliationists

do not take the wrath of God seriously enough. Even though they acknowledge that wicked people will suffer until they repent, they minimize the seriousness of disobedience to God.

On the other hand, I find the eternal torment doctrine even harder to swallow. The traditionalists tell us that people will be gnashing their teeth for a billion years wanting to die, but not allowed to die...pain beyond anything people have ever experienced...and then having a billion years ahead of them...and then another billion years, and then another. I must agree with Dr. Clark Pinnnock that the eternal torment doctrine "... makes God into a bloodthirsty monster who maintains an everlasting Auschwitz for victims whom he does not even allow to die."[14]

What does God have to gain by torturing people forever? Does anyone benefit from that? Is that truly justice?

Traditionalists may shrug this off saying that we, with our puny human minds, cannot say what justice is. God is too big for us to understand, and, therefore, we must only close our mouth in the face of a just God inflicting eternal torment.

I agree that we must stand silent before a sovereign God who is just in all that He does. But it is not sacrilegious to question what will happen on judgment day. Indeed, we are called to think about that day and orient our present lives according to God's final judgments.

So think about it. What is justice? Romans 2:14-16 reveals that God instills within us some sense of justice. Paul encouraged the Corinthian Christians to exercise their sense of justice now while we are in this life, because we will be called upon to judge the angels in the next life (I Cor. 6:1-3). Of course, God is the ultimate judge and we must wholly throw ourselves at His mercy, but we do have some sense of justice

---

14 Clark Pinnock, "The Destruction of the Impenitent," *CTR* 4 (Spring 1990): p. 253.

instilled within our nature by the God who created us.

Does 70 years of sin deserve ten trillion years of torture? Visit a burn center at a hospital. Do the people there deserve the pain they are experiencing? How about that same pain and even worse lasting forever?

Hitler had tens of thousands of people tortured day after day until they could no longer survive. We consider such men evil. Of course, we dare not think of God as evil, nor even cruel, yet the doctrine of eternal torment accredits the most heinous actions to Him.

Who is this God we worship?

When we look in the Scriptures, we see a God who is serious about sin, yet His judgments correspond with the seriousness of the offenses. Yes, God punished sin, but nothing is seen that is as severe as what is taught by the eternal torment doctrine. That doctrine is not consistent with the God who is revealed throughout the Scriptures.

Nor is the view of ultimate reconciliation consistent. God stretches forth His hands all day long wanting people to come to Him, but the Psalm-writer warns us:

He will not always strive with us,
Nor will He keep His anger forever.

(Ps. 103:9)

He will ultimately judge those who continually reject His love.

The view of hell which is consistent with the God who is revealed in Scripture is the view of annihilationism. Wicked people will pay for their sins and then be destroyed soul and body in hell.

Conclusion

Through my study of Scripture I have come to believe that annihilationism, along with conditional immortality, is the most biblically accurate view, completely in harmony with the character of God and the nature of humanity.

In contrast, the traditionalist portrays a sadistic god and takes from Greek philosophy the idea that all people are immortal. The ultimate reconciliationist denies that God's judgment is punitive and that some sins will never be forgiven. It also distorts the biblical understanding of the nature of God and the nature of humanity.

In conclusion, hell is real. It is a place where wicked unrepentant people will be sent. After they have paid for their sins, they will be annihilated because God is just and merciful.

However, I want to soften my position on this doctrine, because a person's belief about hell is not fundamental to the Christian faith. The only doctrines worth being dogmatic about are those which distinguish true Christianity from false belief systems. Our understanding of hell is not one of those doctrines. There are great Christian leaders who have studied the Bible and come to different conclusions than I have. I respect their views and I recognize their sincerity in serving the same God whom I serve. So then, I have done my best to study the issues and I have arrived at what I believe is the biblical view of hell. But if on judgment day, I discover that I am wrong, I will close my mouth before a holy God and thank Him for sending His Son to die for me.

Victorious Eschatology

Co-authored by
Harold R. Eberle and Martin Trench

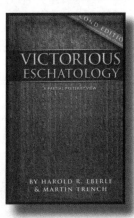

Here it is—a biblically-based, optimistic view of the future. Along with a historical perspective, this book offers a clear understanding of Matthew 24, the book of Revelation, and other key passages about the events to precede the return of Jesus Christ. Satan is not going to take over this world. Jesus Christ is Lord and He will reign until every enemy is put under His feet!

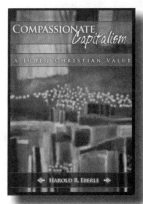

Compassionate Capitalism:
A Judeo-Christian Value

As you read this book, you will learn how capitalism first developed as God worked among the Hebrew people in the Old Testament. The resulting economic principles then transformed Western society as they spread with Christianity. However, our present form of capitalism is different than that which God instilled in Hebrew society. What we need to do now is govern capitalism wisely and apply the principles of capitalism with compassion.

Releasing Kings into the Marketplace for Ministry

By John Garfield and Harold R. Eberle

"Kings" is what we call Christian leaders who have embraced the call of God upon their life to work in the marketplace and from that position transform society. This book explains how marketplace ministry will operate in concert with local churches and pastors. It provides a Scriptural basis for the expansion of the Kingdom of God into all areas of society.

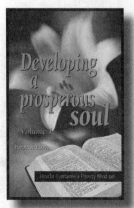

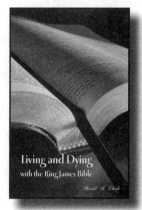

Living and Dying with the King James Bible

The King James Version (KJV) has been a gift of God to the Body of Christ. It has been the standard of truth and inspiration which has stabilized the Protestant Church and blessed millions of people. But someone needs to say it: the KJV is an inferior translation. In these pages, Harold R. Eberle clearly shows the errors and biases of the KJV, hoping you will consider the advantages of more modern Bible translations.

The Coming Judgment
Based on Your Deeds

You have read the Bible verses which talk about God rendering to every person according to their deeds. You have heard verses which talk about various rewards being granted to those who overcome. You want to hear, "Well done, good and faithful servant."

But how can our deeds be taken into account if we will only be judged on the basis of our acceptance or rejection of Jesus Christ? And if our deeds will be taken into account, which deeds will God be looking for? Read this and you will know.

The Spiritual, Mystical and Supernatural

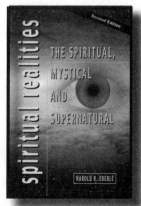

The first five volumes of Harold R. Eberle's series of books entitled, *Spiritual Realities,* have been condensed into this one volume, 367 pages in length. Topics are addressed such as how the spiritual and natural worlds are related, angelic and demonic manifestations, signs and wonders, miracles and healing, the anointing, good versus evil spiritual practices, how people are created by God to access the spiritual realm, how the spirits of people interact, how people sense things in the spirit realm, and much more.